MW01198943

Depleted Burden Down

Deborah Meadows

Depleted Burden Down

Deborah Meadows

PS3577
Factory School, 2009
Queens, New York

ISBN: 978-1-60001-975-3 (paper)
ISBN: 978-1-60001-976-0 (cloth)

Factory School is a learning and production collective engaged in action research, multiple-media arts, publishing, and community service.

FactorySchool.org

Acknowledgments:

Segments from this work have appeared in *New Review of Literature* and *Burnside Review*.

Cover Photo: "coil of nails" Credit: Deborah Meadows

Dedicated to Howard

Contents

Procuratio

How is it that the long draw-down from a set of commonplaces whether first or second, here or elsewhere, an array of parts or the arrangement itself, the divide between meaningful and deviant became irreconcilable in scope and intent to rhetorical devices now become useful to resisters? To be a limit case, one citizen went in for the panel-style tattoo as if artistic tradition woke from a somnambulant press of time, changed horse by post, then changed back as the horse of translation.

Irony and introspective sketches, erotic and religious themes: the color of justice, one could argue, grounded simple conditions.

The fee simple occasion is the subject as frailty comes to be a devotional matter. A day for human rights, subsequent truths and hope, craft not picked up on surveillance monitor. Their daughter, their water is running out. Their conscience renounced beliefs that persecute commoners under pressure: a film showing a schedule of flashbacks, that apparition of series might mean reform, no longer dying in confinement or isolation, the sandstorm for twelve days and nights. Topology, scenes. Thought measured thought hampered by "philistine" as a charge, dice throw as good.

So here we are. But personified figures seem a shrunken sort of reason or blemished intellectual integrity, yet when grandfathered-in, a special standing prevents even application, fortunetelling a war. The urgency of thought, analysis, etc. in their heyday are near impossible to see as style with recognizable features easy to satirize. Even so, who undertakes critique: slave or master?

Who makes news internal?

Could such unions of thought and feeling have built a phrasal immediacy, or, at least in terms of short units of speech whether chant, nurturance, or command:

Go cosmos.　　　Hush child.　　Set digital timepiece to Gregorian mode.

Was it the supposed lack of self-sacrificing cause—here we're not to stint on expense of time toward demilitarization—that we might read analyses of popular items & mass produced toys? We could pick apart the way a product draws from & reinforces orthodoxy while exuberantly sales came in waves & went. For Donne, did not philosophy "call all in doubt," find how a unity might be grasped from scatter?

Then the rain began to fall. I say, did you notice how sunshine has ended? The work has a highly-unified structure, a colonnaded walk, a strip of runway lights receding into storm front. As metalepsis came to be for Quintilian and later rhetoricians, did they find pleasure and order in those sets of association, or truth unavailable to ordinary patterns of thought?

Here are letters and numbers. No grand act to follow with one less grand. No spooky sense of inheritors that never cancels out scratchy and hiss-perforated source of influence in a Freudian comedy of repression undone. To be trapped in the logic of representation disallows what we are here about: minor islands, these desires. A cough or secondary rash—not theme of entropic unwinding here.

But this folding knife, this toad-stabber or father-killer was distributed to all veterans of World War II in bivouacs and colleges, out on the road, and in jars. Truths of that time & place—force of thought, forced to thought. Could echo be distinguished from direct quotation, and further, could that distinction save authorship, originality, things our nationals are good at? Suspense in how the prince of Denmark is revised by the master, yet hasn't the master written our very world? Let us read on and see.

In the socialist ideal, theory met practice, and some of us went to visit varying post-revolutionary moments. In Havana, I was asked why Buffalo poets are not the same as the New York school poets: "Buffalo is in New York, right?"

Like a metaphor that places a word or phrase in a new context configuring new meaning, the situation and the oddity, or its degree of oddity, can reveal intention … so it's said.

A metaphor places a word or phrase in a new context configuring new meaning, the situation and the oddity, or its degree of oddity, can reveal intention … so it's said.

Could mixed vehicles have a tenor:

The spider of resentment. God's pity at the throat, immigrant
mantle of sublime words made by claims to secrete value.

Abhorring a void, the empty place is re-taken, authority run against,
does the engine of nature miss in alternate revolutions? They say
no and mean yes. Why is secular life so difficult to imagine lacking
celebrity? We could be big; we could be gods.

As a technology, can religion do things, produce offspring we consume bloodily? If we might. If we might come. If we might come to know things, perhaps we would not handle them so roughly, perhaps not misinterpret *essence* whenever we're thrown off-track by fictions of origin, genealogical descent.

Yet failing that, might we see and interpret change side-stepping how we too often restrict our talk in terms of opposites as abstractions, so free us to see what is right in front of our noses, blood in the streets? Falsely reconciled: movement of theology into anthropology.

Of self-emptying systems: nihilism. How can "yes" displace "no"?
Sunyata replete.

But a substitution theory: the word for the thing, the thing for the
other thing, has a "universal" appeal. It's money. And little in the
way of theorizing can interrupt its commerce, its erotic appeal.
This rainy heartbreak, that dime-store by the ear of the mob, face
out loud. Keep ocarina far from selvage: blew, then method and
mathematical certainty. Haul and scrape good Word for importation
to godhead, poached and re-set, spring mechanisms and all.
Executed by market track, human capital, finance group, our prize,
seminar on human entourage if you have the software, foundlings'
Houdini, erased land, term professor, robot message. Hard to see
the go-between we are.

No & double-no. Workers know weight of burden— our "reality" enclosed.

Workers know burdens separated from their premises but know, too, principles of production.

Workers know weight's requirement separated from later more distinct consequences. And so, are Christ.

But how does experience of the real reduce it to the cube strapped to my back with twine?

Divisions:

—mutilated ones have heaviest burden, maybe over-interpreted, under-understood, etc.

—an ass that went along with everything, helped justify terms of self-exploitation

—opiate dreaminess is not the recommended way to carry being

Mild lamb of the hour where emphasis fell on the value of
conceptual appeal, how a tender cube might carry allusion, owing
formula to flow … so, matters change, a pagan stance an incorporeal
narrator takes, not to conflate that state with omnivorous childhood
wilds, its youth

/ \

formation   dissipation

There installed: a quantity of prose, citations, stamps (brief, dactylic
and diminished spondees), inscriptions, images (daring and insipid).
Thus is one very different from the protagonist about whom you
read? A peasant habitus—read with cynic pleasure on Horacian
rustic scenes, one Southern winter where dispositions come to be.

Tomcat calls
porous, a bear follows, warm yourself in his hut briefly, same movie
dream-sequence in that work of early days: who sits at the table but
hippogriffs & lion-headed men, goat-bearded giraffes, electronic
peddlers into the bargain taking fifty for two, a common collection
& book in bed looked into causes, interpretations, synthetic
applications and skipped to the lou my darlin'
        to your maker address this conflict: *I feel faint*
Here, alone, our nebulous journey is brief. Born a people, and to die
for that is sad.

Of tubes.
Years of austere reclining, a claim or evidence of falsehood can
be sloppy and correct. A stab or squawk—radio-style—is it moral
indignation? daredevil findings?

Nature, like truth, a silent partner, also named by its case.
Crowding out anonymity, botanic studies deeply invested in
advancing enterprise salient with species of *tube* as transfer means,
duct, structure, old-style vacuum, Modern-made (selfish & on
every corner, a coffee bar), or smooth driving so poles flick by in
recession, rows of corn stalks, other crops, electricity.

Of double-talk. Wandering big world the letter we drive from X to
Y, torus.

... idea enclosed by position, from there, is the still center, master of all at the level of brush stroke, gouache, rag content. That electric sharpener is staring at us. Or at Lacan. On planet earth, light is caught in time-bound meanings as all cities are living museums to greater or lesser extent, contrived vision, style of diorama, golden age, its tarnished sweetener.

Growth in terms of species variation and vitality: how up the city's hill its planetarium becomes cancelled.

What to do with old dusty objects après high water mark of
plunder, repatriated several items held in London, a prominent
collector—city itself—from Egypt.
poof: "purity" gone
poof: "authenticity" gone
Hundreds of jerry cans in petro-chemical dreamtime, theme of
masks and urban-based actors sustained where first "naturalists"
dispatch one hundred birds to study their anatomy, move on to next
life form, then on.

Poetry, where people lodge complaints & can re-assert their
preferences in literature.

Walking—pace as time—sequence acted, re-enacted, stroll exempt from ritual status, an obligation to record stray things not thoughts e.g., route is path not attempt nor their pernicious optimism in Baghdad.

So an image version of language might take up maize that is genetically modified, alienation at home and at work better than a threat of offensive procedures begun with tanks. Whether the ability to express mental images with which "we" may empathize such as "their" plight, wages, and shortages that occur on the Cartesian flat screen that is mind or to purvey a set of resemblances between Lockean ideas and things is not what provokes us to step toward the podium and begin a primary language game.

Before people realized the effect of windblown pollen no fighting broke out and women, for the first time, faced a collection of flaked-stone implements that spoke in the manner of contemporary linguists of propositional attitudes—thought, beliefs, intentions. Depressed, our favorite satirical cartoon understood the off-flow, seepage, and downstream effects, the consequences of a nation's independence, free elections forcibly held between factions that unlike Newtonian gravity were subject to international monetary policy, and so came into fields no matter fenced areas, signs.

But put off principled involvement is not our only shot at rights, so much derived from social practice, so much went without funded scientific determinations too long against unregulated kinds of open pit extraction, conventions that govern what speakers mean getting you to believe and conceive.

The state will be seated here, the church will be seated there emphatically here-and-there is sanctified, made holy, this injustice, decreed from above, cleansed of contemporary images. How extraordinary the ordinary, how formed the reformed.

A picture of a possible state of affairs, one is obligated to give a most charitable interpretation not as a last reaction but a disposition toward there and there-arising, a curtained birth.

It changes you.

This wool: power's propensities, dirt's corrupted results. Let to leave, valve prayer, the wheel of conscious-ventricle undoes itself, little left behind but ramshackle you.

A time plagued by wars and intrigues, the government moved south after invaders took over north, prominent families struggle for power—it is during this period of political factionalism that poets discovered nature's beauty in the rustic quietude of farmland. Measured parts helped rule out strangulation, a language configured how blunt washing never said half-blind, lung.

Dealt a pair, near-full house, range of margin, the round opens clockwise card for card improves things, stick to your reach and raise them.

A formal likeness between rivers and mountains—no mythical animals nor imaginary objects—a verisimilitude dominated taste, emphasized landscape, and later small objects such as fans, screens, musical objects, part of salon life, its notions of high bred ideals, aestheticism.

A wall perforated by age, thus light, a lot of small occurrences unrelated to each other's molecular build. High pollen: the *vous* in use, not your ragweed's stepchild. Frivolous, to critics, works not making use of four tones nor social critique.

Note: I quell myself in you. In response to new musical forms, lyric emerged, and to this day written to tune patterns whose melodies are long forgotten. Could have saved on furnishings, saved from outside's perimeter, cruel history. Of the types of manslaughter, where the hands are macular's vault of semiprecious numeration, grain-count's other body yoked to concurrence, place. How else a post-slavery economy made to re-make pulverized flour, consensus' loan, pork count's back ranked cuts by examiner, packaged on business tables, smoked out and vacated—old melody's purveyor, disfigured swamp child, fell sway of influence, national effort.

Popular lyric met street with practice of literati, furthered
refinement and use of parataxis, curbed tendencies: how our
viewers at home say it's no excuse, we've all had erosion, childhood,
withstood strain recombining cleverness or desperation's
disproportion enjurored by representative's so-called selection, how
our trial changes color by day.

Our twined text makes string, a device's scriptural heap newly peopled with saying, with image, and with images knotted against installment. We might suppose an ideal here, given the crying out against injustice. Down went tyranny's tier, the goods for few go, now conferred-upon these rights' human, upright, bipedal so that all self-sense is present, so unnatural's free of arbitrary's cell.

Nostalgia's jar, jarring still through clubs and social gatherings the abolitionist spirit, consumed boxtop's extruded plastic toy, complacency' easy to carry tote. Porters' paint-by-Soviet wheat tractor's lettering steeply angled red, progress' back-then, our popular base substructures baron's rubber standard, sole-car, retracted touch. Mumble, mumble.

For those who wish to express their undying loyalty, this belonging of waiting man, out of image, or tempera common means; out of stone, temporal wind-down. Wind, water. Foremost solemn face defaced, tree on sparse stage, capacious wooden panel leading into one lead slug, all time.

Desecration of tombs, dank, of dankness sensed, how they get to you through your symbols, register's gullied stone, passage of pilgrims worn into our sonic cave.

Three-part. Figurative, we say, had dilated swimmingly.

Three Considerations:

They had to establish immutability of the book. Cajoled them with things that are come to pass, war—look at who his father is, then who his mother is.

All book divisions of kind and type: fathers instruct sons in virtue, our men learn when to attack, when endure.

A continuum between moderate use of things and contempt; he came from kings.

The debate went between "transplanting" or "inheriting" poetic practice in mainland China, mid-twentieth century that snarled back, grouped map-sense. Where five-matters as thought, our lost continent. Would Euro-emissary measure for malevolent, thus make Du Fu overly scored as ethical equivalent, out from the start?

Beside a cinder heap with sparse tree, Estragon's Von's cart's collection—a parody of ecological, logical bunched plastic bags. Released from annual cell, delivered as set, suspended animation's nomad, mobility's play-back, out where depleted stage makes possible a training video with emphasis on community in "our deserts of California," wealth of descriptors.

The costs, in Ancient Greek tragedies, related to preparing a chorus
were assigned by the state to a wealthy man. In rectangular array
and often military in its sort of movement, a chorus might question
who held identity's change in nomenclature's expression or fist as
leadership-time, the conservative soul of the play.

Our century: a civil cause, virtue on militant cloth or medium
that nips a thin purchase on unrolled spin from the news desk.
Turneresque, no less, in analog funding. Fuel on the wing, soft
cloche, back when *who* has been haze's radiator, a more side-sited
one in mechanism, transfer. Tension of tragic hero and society
played against background of banal opinion and received wisdom.

From where, from where did another come to inhabit a pilgrim's phobia, or phobic take-over out in the woods. As a form of possession, had means a number across will? Low level, frog sawing until out, had said it all subtracting magic.

Well, as a history, hermeneutics opens an arch over time and desire in regard to text and genealogy. In Greek comedy, the ironist is the underdog who might triumph over the strong but boastful one—for Aristotle, a self-deprecating cover of one's strengths that shows taste, restraint. But the philosopher finds both ironic understatement and boastfulness deflections from truth with irony, admittedly, the more noble for its holding from poor taste and narrow advantage.

Socrates, the prototypical ironist. Each poet's identity, its inside bezel supposed to face the hard with facet, part with pyramid, peer with faucet. Unlike Greek tragic irony, against the dark, overbearing forces of fate, state, such an author is absolute ruler over a tiny world, life in accord with the poet's plan. Or for Heine, there is God, the ironist.

Make cowards of us all, the knocked top, vibration's ant dance. Tome, a value per lunk, that fractured stilt, water dip's position on *never*, arbitrary parodic relation to evidence, this-here omission, it's not. There can be overly done coherence between sign and meaning.

The physiology shows main muscle used as language's tribal unplural or type separate from other spine. A burbling forensics maybe, when anniversary's murder is safe from removal, no longer's existence is durable other ways. The day is marked.

Our acts of memory. Full and fine, so thine and blur. Yours' now again. In terms of proprietary behavior: downed tree from other side's guy, untied from prop, disroot, daylight, wire staked from columnar propped "I."

But it ends here without having read traits, judgment's guilt, how forks were taken, chromosomes relieved of that old code cohering as skin on paint.

Quine, the proof

—Quine—

      The car won't start.
      The car started on first try.

It's warm.   It's become dim.
      Our observation, Quine writes, "is the means
of verbalizing the prediction that checks a theory …"
and continues:

           from conditioning?
           from higher language?

1) it's between us, and
2) it corresponds to stimulation

The black swan serves to refute the white-swan theory
        [Is that the only role for observation in science?
               in politics? in logic?]
or, does the sight of a black swan serve to strengthen theory?

—Quine—

                    in language, things are things
when "it" is applied   (even invisible air)
              yet, isn't "it" *out-there*
in the world, old poor language symbolizes?

There exists.
There exists, a context, that is.

sensory: This characteristic goes with that thing
science: Will that thing have that characteristic each
    time?

  To shuck off patrimony of religion and nation.

  The sacrifice seemed a requirement for entrance
      to a larger literary world.

—Quine—

not a thing expressed through variable modes
      but particle as a certain state, *a* or *b*

truth function & predicates = world?

         monolithic sentence, ten-ton rock
         of proxy function

It's about the world & the language we use.
It's about the language we use to express nonexistence.
It's about the language we use to express illusion.

         word—deviated probability
         (seen again)

To learn exhaustively—immersed in human accumulation
      not necessarily saturated with world

Coming into another language, entering wedge

Early Soviet cinema

(Occupation)____liked to discuss fantastic personalities
  with me & political products of his America,
circumstantial letters & galvanized obligation toward episodes,
  frontiers (geographic, and so horizontal, etc.).
Always preoccupied by mixed ethnicity in a way
no other nation could care less about, our
novelist read titles, sagas, emblems, systems
for desperate, closed minds, and how
interchanged codes merit another key.

     *

Sonar, conspicuous

easy snivel, old Penelope
        absorbent

section, three-part
        archetype

beast, ill-defined
woman, a mode.

It follows, return
of man pacified
her

danger pronounced
syllables mitigate
transfer
        parody, dentine

*

spare carts, quick
brushstroke, ravel
           down

*

not here
he gone

*

miasma, olympic

pulsion of cars
          go fulgurant
          around

words, syntagmatic
born-symbol
                    dulzura

*

pico-measure
          truncated
memory, century-aroma

each thing
confluent to prisons'
          harmonica

beat ivories, values
                    vertical
          promissory

— Vertov poems —

… common period by hangar.
How many times the clock has no purpose?
                              In its relation to other

clocks, self-similar row, city by city, exemplar
of un-Bergsonian time; position
a rapprochement between orthodoxy and travelers.

A means to immobilize duration,
claim to make particle, heritage that swell
of memory uncovered by tissue, gesture.

A doomed organism with a movie camera,
plow by rhyme, subtracted-material groove,
the *why* in why our icons mourn, had once.

Dziga Vertov group

"We're winning" at copper logic without
electrification—"lighting the hut for reading"
devices align Tennessee Valley to Kazakhstan

Lenin's speech on industrial goods:
their screen image accretes modernity
paired assembly lines recede in black and white.

At skew, off the pilaster, weight transferred
at lopped interval so a room, beacon, long-playing
quotation run, piano study passed around.

— Vertov poems —

Pokes the air
with his finger
      Trotsky

warrantless
surveillance
passed

on one
side

America
tumbled
on other

turned sideways

neckties
of varied colors
          intertitle

     tumbled
on other side

turned

neckties
of varied colors

pokes the air
       Trotsky
             intertitle

warrantless
surveillance
passed house

on one
side

America
       turned sideways
a sign
of varied colors

with his finger
       Trotsky

tumbled
       turned sideways

on other side
       surveillance

America
turned neckties

with his finger
on one

side

Trotsky tumbled
America

of varied colors
on other   intertitle

turned warrantless
        on one

surveillance
neckties poke the air

America tumbled
sideways

of varied color
Trotsky

warrantless house
on other

Translation, the bass accompaniment

1

The word. Period. Periodization, as a sequential process.

The province of the right point, more exact than dotted points.

This argot like punching adventurers of film, ethnology.

Derived points from Latin, or a minimal extension of "thing".

There are painters who before they paint go across,
        anticipate seeing images across discrimination.

They leave white to the image; they don't go there.

Like a baby's head, they exit pugnacious lines of continuity.

They say the point of making progress converts the line.

But the line, it has not made progress.

Nor has the image.

To be an image is to play at continuity.

To play at statehood.

Absolute progress along a line is to close & make an idea
        found wanting: *ideation, figuration*.

To be the bird you have in your head? Painters have no heads.

2

Three questions on where you place yourself

before you were consumed by life.

We have necessities in the interior city and libraries enough.

The province is a mode of seeing.

We have readings, seasonal winds, prejudicial locals.

I travel to the capital frequently—each year or every two years.

The alternative for the older generation is not ours.

My contacts have been more spacious & our dialog stimulating.

"Heat dilates corpses."

Many from my group have dispersed to France, Spain, Venezuela.
        I came to Mexico in the middle of the intellectual ferment.

The relations between art & life, for me, are impossible to negate.

Verbal material is a dialog with destiny.

Personally I prefer a life distant from literary circles where disputes
        and penalties characterize the place once separated from
        the noise of conciliation.

If something results in a poem—well, that is a miracle.

There is not a formula to repeat it.

Biography

service, First Communion stride
        into the loss
        forbidden to us mortals

little fish that were everywhere, insomnia
        functionary, rabble
        made their origins disappear

like a wild creature, or another person's pillow
        not graduated glasses, or
        this removable cover

probity in the least calculation, pockets
        forced them to return
        spiked with language reduction

the back of cartoon's eyeballs and nose
        from trajectory of a séance
        buzzard, signs, a prophet

still, tenant farmers identified calamity
        an egg one hundred years old
        poor people's lawyer

Opposed to purism and thwarted love, troops
        guided by different smells
        a silversmith's skill

Fruitful trades against sugar-mill attacks
               a thread or secret message
               first to come upon the bay

So unlikely, this recovered data. A stem from which
               we build out an ethical growth,
               substitute for mother flesh.

Arrival

one hundred cigarettes, a daily commentary,
       chip, or cache of favor
       our guard might

make life bearable, swamp of pointless stops
       air not properly sealed
       the phone is not free

churned up mud, mudflat smell, dogs,
       aged-horn, clavé of train-track
       the poet said, inspired what degree

matter-parsed is matter, dull lump
       whether corkscrewed lathe-shavings
       or razor thin gaseous film

resumed offensive without warning, foam
       of nostalgic memories post-date
       how it felt, nitrate remainder

post-rain, chalk flats at a distance, improbably
       powdery close-up, descriptors
       built for containers, centennial parade.

Another interview

Investigate the truth of your time, the work of sputniks.

Let's be precise, no analog, no wooden sanctified tradition.

Human expression in fibers will result in predictable fabrics, so where are examples of the *ignorance-doctrine*?

Mostly, poetry is against having results.

During the last quarter of a century, poetry in this country differs in who has the bad taste to mention capitalism or not.

Half the people worry about where the poetry of our country is going; the other half worry about the status of their dialog with reality.

I agree: to write is to inscribe the world.

There are many realists. So their polemic, "realism," is a bit ingenuous. To pretend to be a photograph is not to accept poetry as the inverse proportion to its informative content—like our times of disinformation, we sit through such at school or how the mass media enters our heads—but the use of certain artifice provokes an illusion of reality.

It follows in what is tactile; its taste and smell are going to be unified and incomparable.

All our good current writers are reticent to be a party or school.

As an alley, "aesthetic" is a poor insult as are political pamphlets which never compare strongly nor become major.

I'm not interested in knowledge about knowledge, or art about art—they are all a trap.

Who needs a trap when we have a state of no functioning signs, violence, exploitation, and alienation?

There is no entertainment industry without a poetry of indignation.

We believe in a parallel universe to Language, yet plunge right into the medium of language.

It is not more important for your listener, this reflexive scene.

Apotropaic Shuffle

Of disagreements on the history and function of the apostrophe, some sources say it's used for missing letters or had a start as a printer's mark to indicate omission, but more interesting is the claim the "cumbersome name for an awkward mark" is rooted in the Greek phrase to "turn away" from the audience when addressing another person.

Still others show mere possession complicated by, perhaps, eight genitive cases. Here we've used it: space constraints in newspapers, compressed words in rap lyric, text message, advertising. Typically seen and not heard, these marks attempt to dispel confusion. Not having exhausted *possession* as cultural insertion of devil into the dance or fervor into rhetoric, punishment into excess, message into the medium, we go on.

Some see the result of homophonic confusion (there's and theirs or it's and its) leading to the death of apostrophe as a required mark in standard English. With time, companies dropped the mark in advertising and street signs. The US Board on Geographic Names has done the same. How to represent speech in written form…

In the strict sense, without importation of non-literal reference, no sleight of hand, no switcheroo of word for other word, or thing for other thing, but straight-up, no chaser.

So, adhere, outside the walls of some Palestine our finite lamp on small motorcycle, paper with rain forecast, vague smell, promulgation of humility all serve to position last properties, poured oil, extracted. We lose all power; nothing to do in shadows. Moving shock, odd frontier in crude letter, that liturgical authority—the demos dead so how advance? what massed weight above this column?

Where there are symbols like renounced lives, our situation in the world is invisible as the poor, mirrored in sentence-construction.

Foreign bits of logic, how in listening to integrated sacred texts from old traditions, death makes passage to painted image modeled on primogeniture of all existence—how things go, congregate, have gone.

As in, ascribed to gravity, this longing for downward, that animistic
updraft of ash or smoke, final cause: God's ways to Man
         meaning in life, a sort of context-dependent
proposition, or not?

John Langshaw Austin's "performative utterances" occur when a
person is *doing* something rather than *saying* something, and he
gives examples: witnessed oath, an apology, ceremonial naming or
conferring, waging a bet verbally, all so the saying is the doing. The
circumstance must exist—one cannot swear an oath alone in the
bathtub, conventions for giving a witnessed oath must exist and be
accepted, he writes. That efficient cause: weight, heat, purpose are
not mentioned.

"Infelicities," Austin writes, include inappropriate circumstances or insincerity, or both, or misuse of performative utterance by a political insurrectionary or wax in your ears, or use in a play, joke, or poem…. Neither radical nor poet, he discusses the performance of [I] "promise that…," but somehow he misses that we report a promise made by a president years back that was both unfulfilled and contingent on the public's short-term memory.

Question now defunct: mind and its location, duration of mind with onset of neuro-finding, and academic philosophy gets re-structured. The Las Vegas mentalist learned there are predictable ways people think from his years as a repair and maintenance man in a Vegas mental hospital. He could predict the number anyone might select from a range of numbers. Each time he dazzled with his ability to predict selections made by volunteers in his night club audience.

He knows, he said in his radio interview, the patterns of human "evolved" brain function, reads them like a book.

If Quine thinks sensory stimuli is all we have "to go on" in arriving at our knowledge of the world, it seems a mentalist could give us the predictable pattern our brains make of those stimuli.

Why the capacity (or, at least, evidence) for self-correction is seen as a feature of artificial intelligence, science as a field, balance in walking.

X lives on the smooth, frictionless plane of scientific observation.

Our innate sequences. Such as they are.

The big question is how we the audience can be so compellingly entertained by the feats of the mentalist.

*

The trick of self-similar growth expressed in systemic theory, how the cool contractions coalesce; hulks and wrecks of old tankers beached for parts, discontinuous topography certainly re-labels smooth welds *junk* and collective identification *ontology of dead ports* sludge-filled locks. Anticipating serial production: cast plaque, necklace panel, harness ornament, jury of peers, the do-right notion of predicate to truth function. It's about the world, the language we use, proxy function. Will that bit of light characteristic of time stand in for theft around us?

Cast as another turn on the "phenomenal," each upside-down perception shocked us awake until *awake* was exhausted, war beat *morphology* into arms, revived ornament's noun, banner's verb, subordination. Having let the excess run-down: predecessor activity to brush-cleaning, spatulate rest.

... on those failures, we'll offer heaven to your slaves, gaudy altars
to dead beauty united by compassion or at least by how contractors
seek their work as a ministry, each a shrink-wrapped modality, a
pledge or irony—here they violate labor law, repeatedly fined. In the
dynamic of loss & memory: free food, housing, tools. A wall welded
to floor irrevocably, surplus keeps wages down in Dubai, Bahrain,
Gulf coast where martyrs to duel homage hired out to other
contractors, endured slurs and police. What objects don't change:
people camp there quartered by reparation, vendors ply an old lure,
government doesn't do much, so rise to snub it there—tracking
unit, dozens of them ...

Other Works by Deborah Meadows:

Goodbye Tissues (Shearsman Press, UK, 2009)
involutia (Shearsman Press, UK, 2007)
The Draped Universe (Belladonna* Books, 2007)
Thin Gloves (Green Integer, 2006)
Growing Still (Tinfish Press, 2005)
Representing Absence (Green Integer, 2004)
Itinerant Men (Krupskaya Press, 2004)
"The 60's and 70's: from *The Theory of Subjectivity in Moby-Dick*"
(Tinfish Press, 2003)